# QuaranTEEN

## Our New Normal

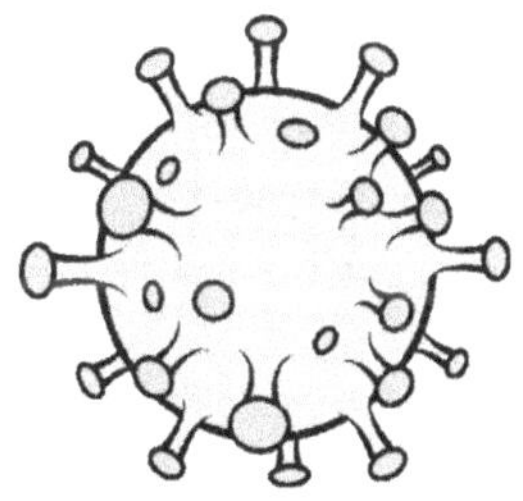

### Nine Teenagers
### Share Their Experiences of
### a Worldwide Pandemic

# Contents


**Introduction**
Kelli O'Brien Watson...................................... 1

CHAPTER 1: **The Perception of Freedom**
Eva Fahrenkrog........................................ 5

CHAPTER 2: **Best Friends are Never Apart**
Mia Conca ........................................15

CHAPTER 3: **God is the Captain**
Brady Durkin........................................25

CHAPTER 4: **Alone Together**
Chris Selvarajah........................................37

CHAPTER 5: **50 Years from Now**
Jeremy Selvarajah ........................................49

CHAPTER 6: **Walking on the Walls**
Chase Lormand ........................................59

Chapter 7:  **A Bright Shadow**
Lauren Kern....................................................75

Chapter 8:  **It Never Rains Forever**
Brooke Holman ..........................................85

Chapter 9:  **It's All How You Look at It**
Helen Treacy .............................................93

# Introduction

**By Kelli O'Brien Watson**

In March 2020, the United States effectively shut down. A new coronavirus, COVID-19, was sweeping the globe, and with no human immunity, everyone was susceptible. The best way to handle the pandemic, according to experts, was to "flatten the curve." That meant that other than people working in essential businesses, everyone else needed to stay home – no social gatherings, no school, nothing. Everyone was told to stay at home until further notice.

Although the unprecedented quarantine affected everyone, there was one group that seemed particularly impacted–teenagers. No longer able to go to school, participate in sports, or visit with their friends, the situation was a significant challenge for them. When Greg, my business partner, and I met in April to discuss business for Scriptor, I floated the idea of creating a project for these teens.

What if we gave them a project that allowed them to focus on something positive, interact with other teens, and create something they could use for college applications and resumes later on? Even more than that, what if they could contribute something meaningful to this very uncertain time in their lives?

That is when the idea for this collaborative book project was formed. Although Scriptor had published several collaborative books before, we had not worked with teenagers, and we had not created a step-by-step process like this one. This was as new for us as it was for the teens, and we all learned along the way. Now, here we are, three months later, ready to publish the book!

The nine teenage authors who participated did not know one another before they signed up for the project. They arrived with various levels of skill and experience with writing and came from different states, including California, Colorado, Illinois, Louisiana, Massachusetts, New York, and Virginia. Yet they were all deeply committed to the task of writing and publishing this book.

Over a period of several weeks, they worked on their chapters, writing and editing the content until they arrived at their final version. They worked together to come up with the book title and cover design. In addition, they all submitted ideas and voted on the charities that will benefit from the proceeds. In just a few short weeks, they became a cohesive team, and this book is the result of their hard work.

As you read the pages that follow, you will experience the quarantine through the unique perspective of these teenagers. You will discover their creativity and learn how deeply they have internalized this moment in time. I think you will be inspired by their deep thoughts and perspectives, and as you come to the end, I believe you will feel hopeful about the future.

Greg and I are grateful to each one of these teens for their hard work and dedication to the project. It was such an honor to work with them!

We also want to thank their parents for trusting us and for their support of every part of the project.

And finally, we want to thank you, the reader, for picking up the book and coming along on the journey.

Now, go ahead and turn the page. It's time to learn how nine teenagers experienced a worldwide pandemic!

# CHAPTER 1

# The Perception of Freedom

**by Eva Fahrenkrog**

"**A**ttention, students: The Board of Education has come to the decision that the school will remain closed until April 7 in an effort to stop the rapid spread of COVID-19 in the state of Illinois."

Our principal's announcement during the last period of the day on March 13, 2020, shocked everyone. The day before, all extracurricular activities had been canceled, and now school was closing for three weeks. Everyone was excited for a three-week break from school. In the hallways, kids chanted "corona-cation" and bumped each other's elbows, which was the new recommended form of physical interaction intended to avoid spreading germs. Back in our homerooms, we waited for the bell to ring and gathered anything we might need for the next three weeks. On the bus, everyone was in good spirits. Some were annoyed about the prospect of make-up work, but still, a three-week break was great. Others talked about leaving early on their spring break trips. Things like this never happened in our town, and I was excited to start my three-week break. Little did I know it would be much longer than that!

The first few days of quarantine weren't so bad. It felt like a normal break. Having the next three weeks off would give me plenty of free time. On the third day of our break, I walked downstairs to find my parents watching the governor on TV. He announced that the state of Illinois would shelter in place until April 7th. Suddenly, we were no longer just staying home from school. We couldn't go anywhere that wasn't completely necessary in order to limit the physical interaction we had with our community.

The governor spoke about the new rules in effect during quarantine: Go places only when necessary, like grocery stores; in public places, wear a mask and stay at least six feet away from anyone else; wear gloves in public to avoid spreading germs. In an instant, our town shut down. Restaurants closed, then gyms, then even the playgrounds. My sister and I were no longer allowed to go shopping. At first, I didn't think it would be an issue because I didn't like running errands, but after two months of being stuck in the house, even going to Target seemed like a vacation.

While we were stuck inside, I felt my mindset shifting. Being trapped on the outside made me feel trapped on the inside. I felt like my freedom had been taken away, and I wanted to get it back. Days felt longer because I wasn't trying to balance school and extracurricular activities. I wasn't focused on getting enough sleep before a test, getting my homework done, practicing instruments, or planning what I was going to wear to school. Quarantine had me tired and confused.

Eventually, our online school program started, so that gave me something to do every day. Seeing other faces helped, whether it was through a video of the lesson or through a group FaceTime with my classmates. It was funny seeing everyone at home. Some people were in bed. Some people snacked on food they grabbed from their kitchens. Getting back to school-work helped my negative quarantine mindset because there was more creative thinking, but it didn't last long.

It became harder and harder to find the motivation to get my work done. Every day felt the same. I woke up, did schoolwork and did my chores. I couldn't get free from the bubble where my thoughts were trapped. I decided I needed to find ways to get back some of my freedom. Over the course of a few weeks, I learned to ride a penny board, made iced coffee, baked new foods, cleaned my room, finished some art pieces, started scrapbooking, and tried a cleanse diet with my mom. After trying these new things, I realized that the shelter-in-place rule wasn't truly confining us. I couldn't go any-where, but I was still free to learn and try new things. Losing things I had before the virus helped me realize how important feeling free and normal was to me. It also gave me the opportunity to find different ways to still have that freedom.

On a warm Wednesday afternoon, I decided to get some exercise and get out of the house. The weather hadn't been great, and I had been inside for a long time, so when we got a nice day, I wanted to take advantage of it. I got my bike and set off onto my normal trail. As I rode through the trees with my music playing and a breeze in my hair, I felt so light and happy, like I could fly. While riding around town, I almost forgot about the quarantine entirely. It didn't matter that I was stuck at home because I found another way to feel both physically and mentally free.

While in quarantine, I missed my friends and family a lot. It was sad to think I wouldn't touch them for so long. The only form of physical interaction we had was an elbow bump. Elbow bumps were no longer a fun joke. Seeing my grandparents, staying six feet apart from them, and only being able to bump their elbows was sad.

When April arrived, I realized my birthday was going to be very different this year. I wouldn't be with my cousins or grandparents, and I wouldn't have a party with my friends. Even though it would be different, I was still excited. My birthday fell on Easter, and I was ready to celebrate both holidays. On the morning of April 12, I came downstairs to the pleasant surprise of an Easter basket and some birthday decorations my mom hung around the kitchen. My dad cooked us all Easter brunch, and then I put on a nice outfit. We weren't going anywhere, but I still wanted to make it special. I got birthday wishes from many of my friends, and my family called to wish me a happy birthday. Even though I couldn't be with everyone, I still felt appreciated. Later I FaceTimed my friends, and we talked about funny things that had happened and things we missed, like school and sleepovers. That night I went to bed feeling happier than I had in a while. Even though we were all separated, I had never felt closer to all the people I cared about.

We finished the school year virtually, along with graduation and awards. At first, I was disappointed, but I had a great year, and I knew I would see all of my friends next year. When the shelter-in-place lifted on June 1st, things started to shift. Little by little, businesses in Libertyville opened back up. Restaurants had numerous safety rules and were all outside, small shops had curbside pickup only, and our farmer's market was at half capacity, but it was beginning to get back to normal. Our community continued to do well through June and July and proved that we prevailed. Slowly and safely, things returned to something that was more normal.

When quarantine began, it felt like so much had been taken away from me, including birthdays, graduation, jobs, vacations, and doing things with the people I love. For the first three months, I felt empty and sad. It was only afterward that I realized how much I learned from the experience. Looking back, I realize that quarantine didn't take everything away, but actually gave me something very precious. It showed me how much every little thing in my life means to me. It made me value what I have and look for the positive things even through dark times. Losing normalcy opened my eyes to how much I truly care about all the beautiful details of my life.

# About Eva Fahrenkrog

Eva's goal for this piece of writing was to record her experience during the COVID-19 pandemic, and she hopes that her writing will serve as a time capsule, preserving this experience for future generations to read and attain an understanding of how it felt to live through the Quarantine. Eva is very interested in history and she enjoys reading personal stories of people living through significant historical periods. She hopes to pursue a career in journalism as a reporter.

Eva gets her inspiration through reading, music, and traveling. Eva found the teen writing project to be educational and fun. She loved meeting new people and was happy to tell her Quarantine story in her first published book.

Eva lives in Libertyville, Illinois with her family and her dog.

# CHAPTER 2

# Best Friends Are Never Apart

**by Mia Conca**

Friday the 13ᵗʰ – it's ironic that this was the date when it all started. It was the day I learned I wouldn't be going back to school or playing any sports that season. However, the reality didn't set in until a little later. At first, I enjoyed the break from all the "go, go, go," but then I became bored. My friends and I texted each other about how we wouldn't be able to play our last games together before high school, and that we would miss making so many great memories. When I realized all the things I would miss, the world around me stopped, and I felt a knot twisting in my stomach. A team isn't just a group of people trying to score more points than their opponent; it's a family. You win and lose together, but above all, you make unforgettable memories together.

It occurred to me that we wouldn't be blasting music together as we carpooled to practice or stopping after a game for a treat. We wouldn't be able to wear matching shirts after winning a tournament. I never thought I would miss waking up at 4:00 a.m. to drive hours away for an early morning soccer game, but I was wrong. On Snapchat, memories popped up from the year before, showing us at soccer tournaments. I remembered how fun it was to sit together late at night in a hotel room, even though we needed to be up and out early the next morning to get to the game.

I also remembered the cold winter days when snow piled up on the parking lots, and I wore so many layers that running became almost impossible. On the sidelines, my teammates and I sat glued together under multiple blankets to keep each other warm. I missed the days at school talking about who would drive to practice and events like "sports day" when we wore our jerseys together. These were the little things that made my team unforgettable, and I missed them all.

Of course, my teams didn't just play together; we also celebrated together, whether it was a win after a regular game or a championship. And not all celebrations were game-related. Sometimes we celebrated something as simple as a birthday. When I was younger, a teammate's birthday meant they'd bring cupcakes to have after a game. Once we got older, we didn't bring cupcakes anymore, but you were still lucky to have your birthday on a game day. It meant you'd be able to hug all of your friends from other towns that you didn't get to see at school. Whether you played sports or not, who wouldn't want to spend their birthday celebrating with people they love? At school, we got each other small gifts, decorated each other's lockers, and sang "happy birthday" at lunch while everyone stared.

But not anymore. When the coronavirus struck, I felt like the world was stuck at a red light. What were we supposed to do now? No more playing sports, making memories, or celebrating birthdays together. At first, I felt like I was stranded in the middle of an island with only my family.

My brother's birthday was the first to arrive, and all we could do was bake a cake and FaceTime with our out-of-town family so we could all sing together. My family sat around our kitchen counter watching my brother blow out candles while our relatives joined in on their screens. It was not that exciting, but it was all we could do at the time.

The weeks passed. Every day was the same as the one before. We sat at home doing online schoolwork. Then, about a week before one of my best friend's birthday, her mom planned a surprise parade, and all of my friends were in on it. The week started with her mom dropping off a cupcake and a big picture of her daughter to take selfies with. We also created a video of a happy birthday message so her mom had time to add everything into a slideshow.

This was not all that was planned for the surprise. On the day of her birthday, we were going to drive by her house. I couldn't wait! I made a huge sign that said "Happy Birthday" and covered it in pictures of us all the way back to kindergarten. Then I added a few balloons.

When it was time, I grabbed my cupcake and sign. My dad drove my sister and me to line up with every-one else a few streets away from her house. There were more than 30 cars lined up and covered in balloons and other birthday decorations. As we drove down her street, I heard cheering and the overlapping honking horns. We drove around her street once and everyone handed her the signs they had made. After going around once, we lapped around again and stopped in front of her house. Since we couldn't all sit around a table together, we needed to improvise and do it from our cars.

This was definitely different, but we made it work. We stood outside our cars and sang "happy birthday" then ate our cupcakes. When everything was over, a few of my friends and I stayed to talk. It was great to see them all, and my friend loved the surprise. Even if we couldn't hug each other or be super close, we were able to make the best of it. It was one of the best days in quarantine. It was almost better than having a regular birthday party.

Little did I know that these parades were going to be the new thing during this pandemic. I participated in more parades for other friends, and some days I even heard horns in the distance as people held parades for their friends or drove around to celebrate the graduating seniors.

My birthday was a few weeks away, and I wasn't sure if there would be a parade. I really wanted to see my friends, but I didn't want all the attention. I kept asking my mom if she planned anything, and of course, she said no.

On one hand, I was relieved that I wouldn't have to stand outside while everyone looked at me waving awkwardly. But on the other hand, I wondered if my mom was just joking or if she really wanted to let everyone have a break from all the parades. I was curious and anxious.

On my birthday, everyone acted weird. I had a gut feeling that something was planned. The day started with a slideshow of my friends wishing me a happy birthday on my TV. It was a great surprise, and I expected to spend the rest of the day with my family. Later I got a text from my grandma that she and my grandpa would stop by. Due to the coronavirus, they couldn't come inside, so my mom set up chairs so we could sit in a circle on the driveway. Why not in the backyard? Everything began to click in my brain.

I heard a horn, followed by a bunch of cheering. One car turned and then another. Soon, all the cars merged and took up the entire street. They honked and blasted, sounding like a badly tuned marching band. My friends hung out of their car windows, handing me huge signs and candy. I smiled and laughed until my cheeks hurt. I was shocked by how many people came and by all the gifts I received. My arms overflowed with brightly colored signs and gift bags. That was definitely not how I imagined my birthday at all, but it was a day I'll never forget.

Quarantine definitely felt like a roller coaster, but it reminded us to cherish our friendships despite these obstacles. It also made everyone more creative. We learned that no matter what happens in the world, we will get through it, especially with friends by our side – or even six feet away. Just remember what Helen Keller once wrote: "True friends are never apart – maybe in distance, but never in heart."

# About Mia Conca

Mia's love for storytelling began as a young child sitting on her grandparent's porch. Her ability to spin a youthful tale woven with imagination and creativity delighted her family on many summer evenings. Seated on a small stool, she would begin, "Once upon a time... "

Mia found a love for journaling over the past few years. She loves to write down everything about her day so she can look back and remember all the great times she has had.

As a student-athlete, Mia now draws her inspiration from her daily experiences both on and off the field. Friendships made and competitions won and lost set the tone for Mia's thoughtful reflection on life as a teen in 2020. In Mia's first writing, her longing to reconnect with her pre-*QuaranTEEN* life is full of emotional highs and lows, which strikes a chord with us all.

Mia lives in western Massachusetts with her family and two rescue dogs, Leo and Bear.

# CHAPTER 3

# God is the Captain

**by Brady Durkin**

You never think about how quickly things can change. For me, in a matter of minutes, I watched the world become something unrecognizable.

**March 13, 2020:**

The day started off normally. I woke to my alarm, hit snooze, and couldn't rise until a few minutes later. I ate something, packed my bags, and left, feeling the cool breeze refresh my face as I stepped outside. When I arrived at school, only one thing was on my mind. Unaware of the events that were around the corner, I thought about my lack of sleep. My partners had bailed on me, so I had stayed up late finishing our presentation. Now I just hoped for the best.

In Spanish class, my partners and I presented about the natural problems in Mexico. As I stood at the front of the room, I noticed people whispering. I didn't know what they were talking about. *Was it me? Did I mispronounce a word?* I knew it was something, but at that moment, I never could have guessed how big it would grow to be. When I finished, I sat down, and my friend didn't waste a second, slapping my arm as he flashed his phone before my eyes. I laughed at the tweet that stated schools were closing.

*No way!* was the first thing I thought. *It must be a lie!* But in minutes, I knew the truth. School was out... for now. Stress crawled up my spine as I thought about my low grade in math, my varsity lacrosse team, my friends... this three-week break would not benefit me. *But then again, it was only three weeks,* I reassured myself. Despite my efforts to stay calm, tension swam through my mind until I felt like it was just me in a boat, drifting away from shore.

## April 29, 2020:

*Quick, close the computer. You're done for the week – finally.*

I closed my last weekly assignment from my online class and bolted from my chair. I went outside, but there was nowhere to go. I could walk around aimlessly or run if I felt daring, but there was no destination. I hadn't seen my friends since school closed. My lacrosse team felt like a memory. All I could do...was nothing. Day by day, week by week, I trudged through the same routine. Sleep in, work out, do homework, go to sleep, and repeat.

Sad? Mad? Scared? Stressed? Bored? There was no one emotion to cover the mixed feelings swirling inside me. I wanted to see my friends, go to school, and play sports, but these normal experiences slipped away. I couldn't find my footing. I was tripping over the idea of never leaving but fearful of returning. I was one of the lucky ones, though. When dark thoughts crept into my head, I escaped to my sanctuary – my home gym.

Growing up in my family, you either exercise... or you exercise. I have worked out my entire life. My dad, Todd, founded the gym Fitness Quest 10, and he has always been there for me. He coaches my teams and encourages me from the sideline. My mom, Melanie, a professor of Exercise Science at Southwestern Community

College, makes sure I enjoy what I do. My siblings, Luke and McKenna, are my best friends, the people I joke and fight with, but can't live without. My grandma, Yia Yia, encourages me to be creative. During quarantine, my family became the only faces I saw.

In my home gym, I worked out every muscle in my body until exhausted. Working out allowed me to release my stress and anxiety. But even with the gym, it was hard to keep every negative, sleep-depriving thought out of my head. News about the virus, death, and destruction was daunting. It often felt like I was stranded on that boat in the middle of nowhere, rocked by waves that intended to dump me out. On the other hand, at times, I was content. I enjoyed waking up when I wanted, watching a movie when I felt like it, and working out as often as possible. I was able to make memories with my family, spend time at my house, swim, sleep, and eat. But these clashing feelings were new to me. I was confused, and I knew I needed to talk it through with my mom.

"Mom?" I walked in front of her and sat down. "This quarantine is hard for me. I don't have coronavirus, nor do people I know, but it's hard. My lacrosse season was canceled, I'm struggling to get my math grade up, and I haven't seen my friends in forever." I let her know the burdens that weighed me down and noticed that as the words flowed out of me, the weight became lighter.

"Brady," she started, "this moment in time is something no one on this planet has ever gone through. So remember, everybody is in the same boat. Everybody... in the world... is with you."

As she said those words, I knew she was right. The boat in the middle of a raging sea held everybody captive, not just me. At that moment, I realized that I wasn't on my own.

"Brady, I want you to promise me something," my mom continued. "Stay close to God. He is the answer."

*Of course, Brady. You are not the answer. You cannot decide the future. That is up to God.*

Like fitness, faith has always been a strong value in my family. I was raised Catholic/non-denominational Christian. My relationship with God drives my decisions, helps me make friends, and sculpts me into the best version of myself. In times of uncertainty, like a pandemic, faith can be tried, but my mom's words reminded me that my future would be something God and I will create together. He provides the path, and I follow. The boat that held us all captive is God's boat. He is at the wheel. Even when I can't see Him, He still works to steer us clear.

After talking to my mom, I realized I had to listen. I had to trust God. I needed to release my stress and do my best. All I could do was get better. As an ambitious person, I needed to not only meet my goals with my hard work but exceed them. I woke up from the trance put on me in quarantine and began the process. I worked my body day in and day out and gave myself optimal recovery time. I put on ten pounds, primarily muscle. I watched videos made by professional chefs and learned how to cook food that tasted incredible. I studied for hours. As a straight-A student struggling to raise a grade, I knew I needed to study. I needed to put in time that normally would go to anything else. With a math test right around the corner, I needed to be prepared. If I aced the test, I would get the A. If not, my grade would remain a B.

*I got this, I got this,* I muttered to myself as I submitted the exam. My stomach fluttered and I felt my heart pump as I scrolled down to see the results. Low B. Since sixth grade, I promised myself straight As. I had kept that promise – until now. This was the first time I hadn't pulled through. My arms turned to Jell-O. My eyes read the number over and over. I hated to fail. I hated giving my all for results that didn't show. Shortly after, my dad walked into my room. "What's up, bud? How did the test go?"

I looked at him but quickly averted my eyes.

He read the room. "It didn't go well? Well, look at me, son." I raised my head. "You desire perfection, but it isn't about that. It's about the learning process. You can't put this pressure on yourself. I love you, no matter what. I don't doubt you or your future. You're okay, bud." He hugged me and left. After a few minutes, I stood and knew what I needed to do: pray and then head to the gym. I walked downstairs and grabbed water from the fridge.

"Where are you going?" my mom asked.

"I gotta work out." I opened the door to the garage and entered the gym. It was late in the day, later than my usual workout, but I needed to be there. I needed to release emotions, thoughts, everything. Afterward, I walked back into the house.

"How are you feeling, Brady?" my family asked.

"Better," I responded and smiled.

## July 10, 2020:

Today, I continue to pray, work out, and make sure I spend time with my family. With the quarantine, I have grown mentally, physically, and spiritually. Looking back, if someone told me as I was preparing to give that Spanish presentation back in March that everything was going to shut down for months, I would have said they were crazy. I never expected such a turn of events. Yet, here we are.

The difference that only a few months made is unbelievable. As well as working on myself, I have kept those who contracted the virus in mind. I continue to pray for those undergoing different problems during this time.

Growing up during these unprecedented times, I feel prepared for whatever is around the corner. This quarantine was a curveball. It unexpectedly stranded me in a boat that made me feel alone. But we have all been in the same boat since the beginning. If we trust in God, we will find our way out of trouble. God's plan may seem crazy, but to get to where we want to be, we must go through the storm. With God as the captain, we are sure to get there.

# About Brady Durkin

Brady Durkin is a rising sophomore at Scripps Ranch High School in San Diego, California. He is the middle child of Melanie and Todd Durkin and has an older brother and a younger sister. Brady is a lacrosse player and was excited to play varsity lacrosse on his high school team in 2020, but unfortunately, the season ended after just four games due to the COVID-19 outbreak.

He also plays football and is hopeful that the football season in Fall 2020 will take place. His favorite position is linebacker, but he plays running back as well. Writing and creating movies, video clips, and short stories is also a passion of his, and the opportunity to collaborate on this book with his fellow writers is a bright light during the uncertain time that 2020 has become.

You can follow Brady Durkin on Instagram @bradydurkin and Twitter @TheBradyDurkin.

# CHAPTER 4

# Alone Together

## by Chris Selvarajah

*"Be faithful in small things.
It is in them that your strength lies."*

– MOTHER TERESA

We played the game of the century! Three of my friends logged on from their homes. No one knew who was going to win the Kahoot. The last question showed up on the screen. I knew the answer and clicked quickly. If I got it right, I won. If I got it wrong, I might never be able to look at myself in the mirror again.

3... 2... 1...

My screen flashed green. I had won the game!

My teacher announced, "Congratulations to Chris! You won some free ice cream sandwiches."

We all laughed. It wasn't until later that I realized these moments created my quarantine memories. The small actions of my teacher, and others along the way, helped me get through this tough time.

It all began on a Friday night when I received an email letting me know that school was canceled. That announcement set off a roller coaster of emotions. It felt like a snow day!

For those of you who have never experienced the joy of a snow day, let me help you imagine it. The day before, you pray with all your might that school will be closed. Some go the extra mile and wear their pajamas inside out and backward. Some people even take a big risk and don't do their homework. There is a lot of superstition surrounding a snow day! When the morning comes, you wake up, look at the clock, and feel butterflies in your stomach because you think you overslept and missed your bus. Then you look at your phone and see that school is canceled for the day. You breathe a sigh of relief and are so happy, you can't go back to bed.

It was exactly the same with the quarantine. When I first heard that school was canceled for the next couple of weeks, I jumped six feet in the air (well, maybe only a couple of inches). Eventually, I settled down, though, because I felt guilty. People were dying each day, and here I was, elated that I could sit back and do nothing.

With each day that passed, I received new emails. As I read them, the roller coaster of emotions continued. First, I heard that spring sports were canceled. Sports have always been a big part of my life, and this was going to be my first year of varsity track and field. I felt upset and frustrated, as if I'd lost a part of me. I figured I could practice by myself and just get ready for the next season. *At least I still have Area All-State to look forward to*, I thought to myself.

Then another email came, and it was the final blow. All music events had been canceled, and ninth-grade graduation was put on hold. But it wasn't just school activities that were canceled. Stay-at-home orders were also put into place across the country. The whole world was in lockdown because of a global pandemic. Sports were canceled, people lost jobs, and seniors lost out on memorable moments all because some person may have eaten a bat. I couldn't believe I was going to be stuck at home with online schoolwork, no sports, no clubs, and no meeting up with friends. It felt like I was under house arrest.

As the days passed by, my attitude became more irritable. It was nothing like I imagined. I thought I would get a couple of weeks off from school and hang out with friends playing video games. I pictured myself sleeping in and catching a movie at the theater. Instead, here I was, stuck inside four walls, not able to do anything. Although I knew things were much worse in other areas, I was frustrated. I watched the news and heard about the unbelievable number of deaths, the loss of jobs, and the hunger around the world. I heard how people were putting their lives on the line to save others, but my annoyance grew stronger. I felt stuck, not knowing how long it would last. It was a hard mood to shake off.

I continued my daily routine – wake up, grab breakfast, check my phone, and do online classwork. I watched shows or played video games. If I got the urge, I ran on the treadmill or lifted some weights. And of course, I heated up plenty of microwavable snacks. Then I went to bed and started the cycle all over again. It felt like I was reliving the same day over and over. Plus, it was the middle of March in New York. Going outside was like stepping into a freezer. This made it so that I had even fewer things to do. If I was lucky, something interesting happened. One time one of my teachers accidentally showed everyone's grade averages. Can you imagine that silly incident being the highlight of the month? But other than those few rare occasions, every day felt the same.

While some of my other teachers were piling on homework, essays, and quizzes, one teacher decided not to give us as much homework. Instead, he did several things to make quarantine better. He made it clear we could reach out to him if there were any concerns about school, COVID-19, or other issues. He made a Bring Your Pet to 'School' Day, where we all showed our pets to our online classmates. There was also Childhood Picture Week, where we shared an awkward, embarrassing, or cute picture of ourselves when we were young. Cartoon Week was fun, too, because we changed our profile pictures to our favorite cartoon.

One day, he decided to make a separate Google classroom with interactive activities. His thought was to create a forum where we could talk about managing time, balancing schoolwork, managing stress and anxiety, and discussing the impacts of the shutdown. He also wanted to include some fun activities like online games, music performances, joke sharing, scavenger hunts, and cooking lessons. At first, I didn't want to do it. But my mother reminded me that I had nothing else to do, so I joined just to say I did it.

The first meeting started off with a talk about stress and how to control it. Then he taught us how to make French toast. Mine turned out great. Unfortunately, I can't say the same for everyone else; one person got their toast stuck in their pan. We cracked jokes, and before you knew it, an hour had passed. In the end, we made it a competition and voted on which one was the best. It was the most fun I'd had in a long time.

He continued hosting these meetings, and we made something new each week. We also discussed important topics, like time management and schoolwork. He added in some sports trivia games and Disney movies as well. I started looking forward to these meetings. It's crazy how these small things made me think of my teacher in such a different way. Before, I just thought of him as relaxed, funny, and good at teaching. But when online school started, he went above and beyond to make sure we were okay. I recognized that he genuinely cared about his students and was a sympathetic person. Whether he set up a meeting to teach us how to cook or created trivia games with prizes, he always made quarantine a little more fun. It's not something he *had* to do but rather *chose* to do.

I started to feel better. The weather warmed up and I could get outside, which helped my spirits. My grand-mother, mom, and sister also started gardening. My grandmother doesn't actually live in New York. She lives in Toronto, Canada. Unfortunately, she came down to visit at the wrong time.

My grandparents came down for my brother and sis-ter's birthday in March. When my grandfather returned to Toronto, my grandmother decided to stay for a couple more weeks. In those two weeks, everything changed. The US-Canada border closed, and she was strand-ed here. Meanwhile, my grandfather was now alone in Toronto, figuring out how to manage on his own. I knew my grandmother and mom were both worried. They were doing everything they could to get her back to Toronto. But as weeks passed and the border remained closed, I overheard them talking about how he needed food and was ordering takeout a lot. They worried he had no one to take him for walks to get his daily exercise. Luckily, other people stepped in to help. Uncles, aunts, and neighbors brought my grandfather food, called him to make sure he was okay, and took him for walks. Even though it might not seem like much, those small things helped out a lot. It definitely relieved my mom and my grandmother. They felt much less stressed and were calmer. Once, my mom even offered to wash my plate, which never happens. That may not seem significant, but it was as rare as winning the lottery for me.

When I saw how small things made such a huge impact, I decided to volunteer at the food pantry. I had done this before, and now they needed younger people to step in. The first day, there were so many cars lined up to pick up food that I instantly felt grateful for what I had. As I placed boxes in people's cars, I heard muffled thank-yous through their masks. Although I couldn't see their smiles, I could see it in their eyes. Helping others gave me a sense of happiness that is hard to describe. It opened my eyes and made me grateful for the experience. Observing how this pandemic impacted people motivated me to continue to help and volunteer my time.

As I sit here writing, we are still under the quarantine. I still can't play a game of basketball with my friends. I still wake up and binge-watch old TV shows, but the sunshine is peeking through the curtains, and my mood has lifted. Being in quarantine began as a nuisance and an interruption in my life, but slowing down has opened my eyes.

Dr. Martin Luther King, Jr. once said, "If you cannot do great things, do small things in a great way." This quote rings true right now. Am I going to find a vaccine for COVID-19 and stop this pandemic? Probably not, since I'm a freshman in high school. But I've learned the joy of contributing to my community. Even though a small action seems like nothing, it means more than you think. A smile or a compliment might just make someone's day. Soon enough, things will become more normal, and what I will always remember from this time is that even small contributions make a big difference.

# About Chris Selvarajah

Christopher Selvarajah is a teen writer who has a combination of wit, compassion, and adventure. He loves reading and writing stories based on realistic fiction, which is what you will find in his contribution to his first novel. He won a New York State Regional Reflections Literature Award for his writing work in 2018. He currently lives in upstate New York with his three siblings and parents.

Christopher enjoys composing rhymes with his love of music. He has been playing both the piano and the viola since the age of five. When he's not attending his daily classes in high school, you can find him dribbling a ball on a soccer field.

You can follow him on Instagram @chris_selvarajah.

# CHAPTER 5

# 50 Years from Now

**by Jeremy Selvarajah**

"Grandpa! Grandpa! Were people actually afraid to run out of toilet paper?" my grandson, Billy, asked as he ran over to greet me. It had been 50 years since the coronavirus wreaked havoc on our country, and today my grandson learned about it in school.

I turned my eyes toward him, and he saw the conflicted emotions on my face. "What happened, Grandpa?" he asked, suddenly worried.

"Although it is true that many people were scared to run out of toilet paper, having to go into quarantine was actually pretty scary," I replied.

"What do you mean, Grandpa? You were lucky because you didn't have to go to school!"

"That's true, but it also meant I couldn't see my friends anymore. And the worst part wasn't that we couldn't see people, it was that we saw the same people all the time!" I said with a smile.

"What do you mean?" Billy asked, confused.

"During quarantine, we only interacted with our family. That was hard for a while, but believe it or not, it actually ended up being the greatest thing to happen in my life. Would you like to hear more of the story?"

Billy nodded eagerly. I motioned for him to sit down next to me on the front porch swing. He leaned against me as I closed my eyes, taking a moment to pull up the memories. Slowly, I began to share my story.

Quarantine began in March 2020 when snow still covered the ground. One day I took my dog, Coco, for a walk. As I started walking, I shivered. It felt like something was off. I pushed the thought aside for the moment, watching Coco trot along the road. Looking around, I saw the houses in the neighborhood and the trees swaying in the distance, but something was missing. I half expected something to jump out at me.

Soon, I realized what was different. My neighborhood felt eerily calm. There were no kids playing basketball in their driveways, no families out for a walk, not even a single car drove along the road. It was so quiet you could hear a pin drop. That was when I fully realized the impact of the coronavirus. People were forced to stay inside and were afraid to even walk out their front doors. Being inside and together all the time was hard, but it changed my relationship with my family forever. We were always close, but that time together created long-lasting memories.

One of those memories happened when I came up with the great idea of having a tug-of-war match. It did not take a genius to see how bored everyone was, and I thought it would be fun.

"Let's have a tug-of-war match," I declared.

"Sure," everyone replied.

Then I jokingly asked, "Mom, do you want to play?" I expected her to say no, like every other time I asked mom something.

*"Mom, can I go to a movie?"*

*"No."*

*"Mom, can I go to my friend's house?"*

*"No."*

While it was possible for my mom to say yes sometimes, when it came to exercising with us, it was nearly impossible for her to agree. So, it made it all the more unbelievable when my mom replied, "Sure!"

My jaw dropped. I did not expect that answer, and as I looked around, I could see that my dad and siblings didn't expect it either. "What? You're kidding, right?" I asked.

"I'm serious," My mom replied. When I later asked her why she said yes, she said she had no idea, but she was glad she did.

As we went downstairs to gather the rope and make the teams, we realized it would be impossible to have fair teams. Whoever had my dad would automatically win. Although this minor problem caused some issues, we did not let it stop us from having fun. After trying to find even teams, burning our hands from pulling too hard, and lots of water breaks, we eventually decided to stop. What we all realized was that even though we had to be with our family all the time, it didn't have to be a bad thing.

We started to find other things we could do together as well, like family movie nights. Movies were something we all enjoyed, but when movie theaters shut down because of the quarantine, we decided to start a new tradition. Every Friday night, we sat down together and watched a movie. While this sounds simple, with a family of six, it was almost impossible to agree on a movie. My sister wanted to watch Disney princess movies, my brothers wanted to watch action movies, and my dad wanted to watch detective movies. We usually just picked something random. They weren't always good, but they did get everyone laughing. Movie nights almost always ended up great, not because of the movies, but because of the time we spent together.

We also enjoyed sports and outdoor activities, which were fun and kept us in shape. When everything closed, including spring sports, gyms, and community pools, I felt devastated. Not only did I lose a soccer and track season, but I knew the chances of staying in shape were slim to none.

Then my brother suggested doing family workouts.

At least once a week, one of us chose an exercise to do. We decided what music playlist to listen to and motivated each other to do the best we could. We tried our best to do this every week and to always finish the workout, but of course, things happened. My father played songs from the "good old days" that we'd never heard of before, and so my playlist became superior to everyone. My mom changed every single exercise to make it easier and took a break every two minutes. And then there was my sister. She woke up every Sunday morning, promising herself she would finish the workout. She said she wouldn't watch TV until she finished. Inevitably, halfway through, she left to watch TV on the couch.

The other extreme was my brother, who gave 110% at the beginning of the workout, and nearly collapsed trying to finish it. Once again, despite the unsuccessful workout attempts, the times we spent together brought our family closer. The jabs and teasing that occurred were funny and kept us laughing and coming back for more workouts, week after week.

In a pond in our neighborhood, the ducks swam in a line, every single one following the leader. When my family decided to start riding our bikes together, we formed our own line. We started off just riding up and down the big hill in our neighborhood. Then my brother started following me on his bike. At first, I thought he was trying to annoy me, so I ignored him. Then I decided to make things challenging for him. I went uphill, then downhill, making quick turns. Soon my little brother followed me, and then my sister and my dad. We played follow the leader on trails and in parks and anywhere we could ride our bikes. Another memory was formed.

Before quarantine, my family never had time to do these activities together. We were all busy with school, sports, activities, and work. But those small things ended up being something we all enjoyed.

"Wow, Grandpa, you went through all of that with your family?"

"Yes, Billy, I did. Although something might seem bad in the moment, you can always find a way to see the sun in the darkness," I said.

"Can you stop speaking in riddles and tell me what that means?" Billy asked.

"What it means, Billy, is you can always choose to look at the positive rather than the negative in a situation. Many people sacrificed their time and freedom during quarantine in order to help the nation become safer. But everything was uncertain. We had no idea how long it would last or if things would ever get back to normal. In the end, I got something out of it that I have carried in my heart for all these years. Before the quarantine, my family was important to me, but our lives were so busy with work and sports that we didn't spend much time together. The quarantine allowed us to re-introduce ourselves to our own families. There were challenges, and we did have moments we wished we lived continents apart, but at that time, we only had each other. The moments we had during quarantine could not be taken away."

Billy sat quietly, thinking about what I said.

"If you want to hear more, Billy, you should ask Uncle Jacob and Aunt Cecilia about our trampoline adventures. They would love to tell you about those!"

# About Jeremy Selvarajah

Jeremy Selvarajah fell in love with reading books as a young child. He enjoys reading fiction and fantasy thrillers. This lured him to writing his debut novel. His conviction in faith and family is self-evident and comes across in his writing style. Jeremy has won multiple Reflections literature awards in the Leatherstocking Region and the New York State levels. He lives with his twin brother and family in New Hartford, New York. His second love – playing modern contemporary songs on the piano – goes hand in hand with his love of playing the game of soccer.

You can follow him on Instagram @jeremy_selvarajah.

# CHAPTER 6

# Walking on the Walls

**by Chase Lormand**

Fin opened his eyes bitterly; he hadn't had a dream. He sat up and stretched, sore from sleeping on the creased flowery wallpaper. It was peeling slightly near his ankle, itching and tickling him as he yawned. Rolling his shoulder, he looked around the house. The lights were off, but a warm light poured in through a window near him.

*No one is home,* he thought.

Crawling over to the window, he scrunched his eyes, looking down over the trees jutting sideways out of the ground and the sky extending much farther below. The only thing that proved time passed was the slight rustling of the leaves. Everything else was and had always been the same. Thinking back, Fin couldn't remember being anywhere other than the wall.

Fin sat with his legs dangling into the hallway. He found the doorframe comfortable, supporting his knees. As he stared off, the wall lamp near him sighed.

Fin rolled his eyes. He knew what it was thinking.

"When will you ever quit staring into space like that?" it questioned. "Especially while blocking my view of that gorgeous painting! Honestly, pick a new spot to mope. I can't focus!"

Fin snorted, looking over at the painting in question. It *was* good, but the frame was slightly tilted to the right. And that lamp had never seen another painting to compare it to.

Fin asked why the lamp didn't just watch the people on the floor like he did.

The lamp grimaced, responding, "They don't interest me. Too noisy. I find the painting much more appealing."

Its lightbulb flickered in excitement. "The preservation of that single moment – it brings much comfort to me."

Fin nodded knowingly, as familiarity and comfort were very powerful, but he was still stuck with a lingering unease. *It's crooked*, he thought with a frown.

At any rate, he moved to the other side of the lamp, if only to quiet its grumbling. Resting his chin in his hand, he watched as people scuttled about on the floor. Fin couldn't hear them, although he saw their mouths constantly moving and calling to one another. He didn't think he was deaf, though. Fin could hear the wind, but it never wanted to talk to him.

As he watched, one of them, a burly man, moved off the sofa and walked perpendicularly over to the small kitchen area. Another one, a smaller child, excitedly fluttered his jaw, to which the man nodded. He was good at predicting what they were saying and who was talking. Soon, a pleasant smell wafted through the house, making Fin's mouth water and his stomach grumble in envy. He looked away, moving back to a window.

Droplets of moisture joined Fin in looking through the window. He hadn't seen any rain, though. Today, a chrysalis had appeared on a small branch. Fin winced, knowing what it meant for the caterpillar inside. He hated the caterpillars before because they wrought destruction on the growing sapling's leaves. After watching them transform, however, he sympathized with their struggle. He doubted they truly wanted to hurt the plant, nor did they want to be trapped in a chrysalis.

Fin knew the truth. When the evening light came through the window, it provided the perfect angle for him to see through the translucent shell. However, there was no caterpillar, just a writhing, semisolid mass. Thus, he pitied the caterpillar, knowing what hardships it would have to endure in order to emerge as a butterfly.

Fin wondered if that was how the people on the floor felt about him. He tried his best to stay out of their way, but some disturbance was always inevitable. He was most likely the caterpillar to their healthy plant – a creature who only fed off of the home it cultivated. Did they pity him, or was he still an annoyance? A fat caterpillar crawled on the glass of the window. Suddenly irritated, Fin flicked it off.

Fin walked around the walls to the back door. Twisting the knob and pulling upward, he crawled out onto the brick exterior of the house. Shutting the door, he squinted his eyes at the sudden light. His stomach continued to growl. The sun was high, and the flowers had all turned to receive its warmth. Fin headed to the tomato planter that sat on the wall near the bedroom window.

One of them was there, a girl this time, who had a trowel in her hand and a sun visor on her head. She turned upon his entrance but did not react otherwise. Fin sat near the planter and inspected the small cherry tomatoes dangling off the vines. Only the deep red and juicy ones were good to eat; the orange and yellow needed to be left for a few days. Fin was careful not to bump the girl as she planted some new seeds in the enclosure. The bricks were rough and uncomfortable, but the tomatoes made it worth his time. Their tart and savory flavors exploded in his mouth as he bit into them. He was the only caterpillar allowed to eat these plants. The girl never tried to flick him away.

*The living room is much too dark*, Fin thought. He was observing them again – a taller, curvier woman, a small boy, and a lean man. They sat on the sofa facing Fin, who was ready to move out of the way in case they turned on the lights. The man stood and stretched, which excited the child. Suddenly interested, Fin sat up. He hadn't been paying attention to their conversation before that. The man stooped in front of the fireplace, setting the dry logs ablaze within. Fin closed his eyes, enjoying the warmth and the crackling sounds emanating from the hearth. He loved the idea of fire. It could take musky old logs and transform them into smoke and heat. They suddenly provided comfort to all in the room and were free to fly forever out of the chimney. Perhaps Fin should set himself on fire. It would be wonderful to be important or loved, if even for a moment. Perhaps he was already burning. The pain was already so great that everyone stayed away. Somewhere, a caterpillar squirmed.

The heat became suffocating all of a sudden. Fin left the living room to think. He pondered for a bit on where to go, and decided he wanted to watch the wood escape; perhaps he wanted some hope. Climbing to the roof always meant a certain fear. The uneven and slanted roof was difficult to traverse, but he managed to slide near the opening of the chimney. A tuft of nervousness bloomed in his throat. Somewhere, a caterpillar began to gnaw on it. He settled in, a fan whirring near him, and the wind blowing steadily. Fin watched as the smoke slowly spread out so thinly that he couldn't see it anymore. Was it still there? Maybe non-existence was the price of freedom. He would probably never find out. Laying back against the chimney, Fin looked out at the twinkling stars. He counted them until the heaviness of his eyelids outweighed his desire to continue.

Fin slept soundly but had no dreams. He wished it didn't bother him. Turning his head and massaging his shoulders, Fin wondered how he slept so well on the uncomfortable tiles of the roof and brick of the fireplace. Smoke no longer came from the fireplace, which felt fitting somehow. The last ember of hope had cooled within him also.

Fin looked out over the sky again. It was the same blue. He didn't normally sleep on the roof because waking up to the abyss usually perturbed him. He was sickened by the sky, but as much as its ambivalence put him off, he was unmistakably drawn to it as well. All those days, thinking of butterflies and smoke and people, Fin thought maybe they were also pulled by the sky. He didn't want to remain on the wall, either. He considered this option. He didn't know if he could jump into the sky or if it would free him from the wall. He was too scared to try.

The fan next to him chuckled, "I think you would like it, you know."

Fin looked over, distraught.

The fan paused for a moment, clattering, "You could let go of everything, everything you cling to – the wall, regret, hope, pain, change. The sky is vast and infinite but empty. You would have no existence to fret over anymore."

Fin wrinkled his nose but weighed the idea. He thought about it but was still uncertain. The wall wasn't all bad; Fin liked the tomatoes. The fan began to get irritated and said, "You should take your chance! If I had legs to jump or freedom to move like you do, I would've been gone already!"

Fin grew more uncomfortable. He didn't like this. The fan felt more and more as if it were his own mind, egging him closer and closer to the edge of the roof as if it were a piece of his own mind, the part he feared and pushed away.

"Perhaps," said the fan.

Fin looked over at him, then huddled into himself.

Fin sat for what felt like hours, hiding his face from the light of the sun and the blue of the sky. Once he was ready to face the fan again, he would turn. The only feeling he had was the wind, but this was bone-chilling rather than gentle. Fin was awash in the cold, pinpricks crawling over his whole body. Maybe this was how the fan felt, having to sit out every day and night on the roof and dream it had the strength to jump.

Fin turned and looked down the sloping roof. The sapling's branches barely peeked over into his line of sight, revealing a shriveled, erupted chrysalis. The caterpillar had weathered this too, without strength or defense. Fin marveled for a moment at its escape. He was still stuck, left to slowly churn in the endless expanse of time and grief and pain that was the wall. He had no choice but to believe that he too would emerge one day, to think that he couldn't escape, and maybe even to not dream. *I must accept it*, he thought.

A butterfly landed on Fin's arm. He had never been able to hear them, or maybe they couldn't talk to him. He looked up at it. An icicle fell from his eye, cutting a gash in his cheek. It fluttered around his head and landed on the fan, which had stopped whirring. Fin hadn't noticed. He heard the fan in his mind. *It's different now.*

Fin continued to cry.

Fin woke up empty, but inside this time. The wallpaper was still peeling, annoyingly itchy. He would have waved hello to the lamp, but he couldn't hear it anymore. He just knew. Maybe he was feeling more like himself. He rolled over and looked into the kitchen. One of them had left their lunch on the counter. It was old.

The water had small bubbles in it. The bread looked untouched; it was stale. Fin's eyes darkened.

*Have my friends died, or did I kill them?* he wondered, although he knew the answer.

Fin moved over to the window again; maybe the sky was a better place after all. He drew the blinds. A caterpillar squirmed behind his eyes.

Lying there with his eyes closed, he heard someone enter on the floor. Fin didn't turn like normal. He pretended to be dead. The thumps of shoes against wood echoed around the house, eventually stopping near Fin and the window.

"Could you open the blinds? I would like to see outside."

Fin turned over, thinking he was mistaken.

The man repeated, "Fin, could you open the blinds? It's dark in here."

Fin turned and stuttered, "How... do you know my name?"

He cocked his head and smiled, "You can hear me, then. I'm Aidan."

Fin opened the blinds, smiling. The empty chrysalis stirred and fell from the sapling outside.

They all surrounded the fireplace. Fin asked if they could light it. Everyone thought it was a great idea. He sat and chatted with them from the wall, but he wasn't alone. Aidan sat on the rug with several of the others. Fin hadn't formally asked for their names yet. They all seemed to know him, though. Fin watched them with renewed interest, soaking in every new sound with glee. The fire crackled over it all.

Fin could feel logs in his chest becoming lighter. His heart may well have drifted into the sky. He shifted and felt a crinkling in his pocket. Putting a hand in to investigate, he found a crumpled piece of paper with a poem he scratched onto it. He didn't remember writing it, but he knew every line already.

*Leaving my shoes by the door – I left my existence to thee*

*Nothing but footprints trace my life*

*What could have been – I won't ever see*

*A flower, delicate wing, curl of smoke*

*Alas, it was all a dream.*

Fin chucked the poem into the fire, smiling as it burned. Its remains would reach the sky and be free from him as well.

Fin bid everyone good night and smiled when Aidan waved to him. The wallpaper itched as he lay down, but he relished the feeling. The others on the floor slowly left the room after the fire was out. When it was fully dark, he closed his eyes to sleep. A single butterfly tickled his stomach in excitement. Fin dreamed about the sky.

# About Chase Lormand

Chase Lormand is a 16-year old born in New Orleans, Louisiana. Oldest of three with two younger brothers, he is a leader and a creative soul. Passionate about art, piano, chorale, reading, and writing, Chase has always been absorbed and inspired by the arts. These talents and skills have been rewarded in the past, as well, with him having won city and state awards for his artwork and yearly participation in the New Orleans Honor choir. Imaginative by nature, Chase has always loved reading sci-fi and fantasy novels, which is well represented by his chapter. He hopes to allow the reader to follow him through a small fragment of his vast imagination.

In the future, Chase hopes to pursue a degree in neurology. While the current quarantine hasn't allowed for a thorough search for a college, his hopes are still very high. As his chapter suggests, it is possible to derive hope from within oneself, no matter the bleakness of one's surroundings.

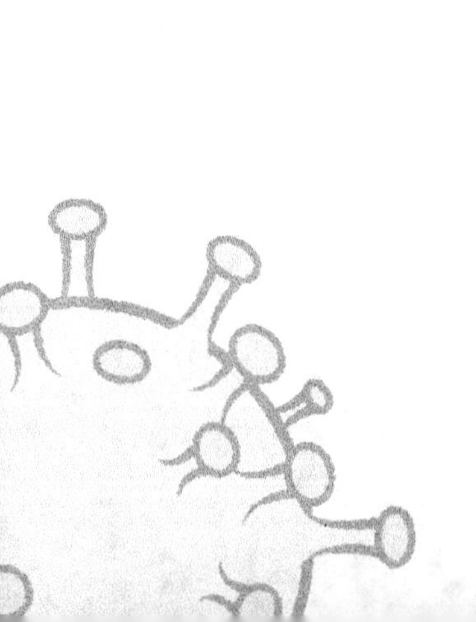

# CHAPTER 7

# A Bright Shadow

**by Lauren Kern**

*Parlez-moi dans un nouvel endroit.* Speak to me in a new place.

*Parcourez une route différente.* Travel a different road.

*Et découvrez tout ce que vous pouvez accomplir en étant simplement vous.* And learn about all the things you can accomplish by simply being you.

Take the road less traveled because it will help you endure in times of crisis. As the world shuts down, you will find a way to speak to others, even if it's not physically possible. Freedom blooms in a world filled with emptiness, and as the world darkens, others find ways to light up the sky. We learn to deal with a crisis that has never happened before. We take the road less traveled as we find new ways to interact without physically touching.

Now I see my friends through a phone screen as we talk and draw together. On FaceTime, I sketch abstract shapes and random characters while I talk. Laughing together and smiling, we long to talk in person. Cristina holds up a sketch of a poorly drawn tiger, and both Lucy and I crack up at the awkward, twisted lines on the notebook paper. They then laugh at me as I hold up my own squiggles – a couple of eyes, a poorly drawn dog, and some random shapes visible on the scratch paper. All of us laugh. Eventually, we calm down, turning our eyes back to the pencils and pens on the paper.

"I really wish I could hug you guys," Cristina says quietly.

"Yeah... me too."

"Same," I agree with a soft smile. I do miss being able to see someone and not have to avoid them like they're carrying the plague. Giving a wave is awkward when I see someone I know but can't go over and give them a quick hug or at least a high-five.

"Same here," Lucy agrees, quieter than before.

I think we miss physical contact more and more by the day. I'm not surprised. It's been two months and I haven't touched anyone other than my mom, dad, and brother. I don't count the neighbor's dogs! Even then, I hear, "Make sure you wash your hands!" after I come inside. We'll see what happens when the world gets past this pandemic/quarantine, but for now, I can only talk to my friends without physically being by their side. We are walking a different road, the pandemic road. It is a lonely, six-feet-apart, stay-away, redefined road that twists into a downward spiral of solidarity. It has taught me that many things are not cherished until they are gone. Touching is one of those things. Hugs and affection keep you close. But now, you're not allowed to come close to someone anymore.

"Social distance."

"Back up."

"Six feet apart."

"Wear a mask."

"Don't get too close!"

"Wash your hands."

"Keep away."

"Can you back up a little?"

"Do you have your gloves and mask?"

"Stay safe."

There is a feeling of anxiety out in public and boundaries everywhere. It makes me feel so alone, even surrounded by people. We all walk together, forced to share a common path that we didn't know was coming. This path is different.

Everyday life used to be beautiful, filled with green forests, flowers blooming, and laughter ringing through the air. Shopping centers and stores bustled with activity. But now it's a different story, a different path, where reality melds with fantasy. It feels dream-like. This is nothing like the beautiful green and eccentric colors of nature. The world has gone silent. It's suffocating. I don't want this. I never asked for this path, but I can't fight the path beneath my feet. I have to accept it.

The change was sudden, but humans are made of something special, a special kind of unity and bravery that comes out in times of crisis. Recognizing this, I sense an opportunity to look within. There is still life.

I can't always see it, but I know it's there. In the darkness, there is light. The ebony sky fades to a soft gray as the sun rises every morning. The earth breathes. Life adapts.

The smallest things soon become the most consoling – FaceTime calls, late-night chats, joyous laughter, cheesy drawings, and when my friend laughs so hard she falls off the bed. Those moments connect us. They lead us down a path of happiness. Sometimes the darkest nights lead to the brightest days. I hope to create a light to guide others through the darkness of the quarantine.

In just a few short months, I've adapted. I've kept going. Through quarantine, through life, it will be all right. I have a plan. I have hope. I have a life ahead of me and people who support me – my family, friends, and neighbors like Mrs. Anne. She's 78 and is always willing to chat with me across the street, even during quarantine. When I go out to water the plants or check the mail in the morning, she is there.

"Morning, ma'am," I call, and she waves and smiles.

"Morning, Lauren. How are you? It's going to be hot today," she says and turns off her garden hose.

"I'm well. How are you? How's Mr. Ryan?" I ask as I grab the mail from the mailbox.

"We're good. Mr. Ryan's staying out of the sun." We share a laugh together and chat for a little while before Mom pokes her head out the front door to check on me.

"It's good to see you, Mrs. Anne. Stay safe. My mom wants me back inside," I say kindly, and she shoos me off with a big smile.

The conversation brightens my day.

Later that day, my mom sends me outside to go for a walk just as Mrs. Anne's cream-colored 2005 Chevrolet pulls into the driveway, its tires squealing. She gets out slowly and waves. The rusty trunk pops open, revealing white plastic bags. She picks one up, carries it into the house, and returns for another. One by one, she picks up the heavy bags, struggling. I decide to help. Running inside my house, I grab a mask and gloves, and I pull them on as I jog across the street. Taking two bags into my hands, I smile at Mrs. Anne behind my mask. She returns my smile with a bright one of her own. I enter the familiar house and place the groceries on the counter, being careful not to touch anything before grabbing more bags from the trunk. After all the groceries are in the kitchen, I return to the driveway, stand at a good distance, and peel off my gloves.

"Thank you, sweetheart," Mrs. Anne calls to me from her doorway.

"Of course, Mrs. Anne. Have a good day." I wave goodbye and continue with my walk.

Mrs. Anne is kind, with a warm smile and a big heart. Her husband is just as kind, with a loud laugh and a playful attitude. Even quarantine boundaries cannot entirely prevent us from helping our neighbors.

We're all struggling to understand what's going on, how to act, what to do, and what measures to take. But as long as we remain open to each other, we travel this new road together. During this powerful moment in history, as the world unites through all the chaos, terror, and isolation, we find and create something beautiful by accompanying each other. In unity, we will endure.

This road is unlike any other, but I am grateful to live in such a memorable time in history. It might feel dark right now, the sky an awful ebony color, but sunrise will come. I don't know what will happen when quarantine ends, but I do know one thing – I lived through a pandemic. And during this moment of history, I stood next to friends, family, and neighbors as we accompanied each other on a twisted path. How many people will get to say that?

*"The beauty of life is, while we cannot undo what is done, we can see it, understand it, learn from it, and change so that every new moment is spent not in regret, guilt, fear, or anger, but in wisdom, understanding, and love."*

- Jennifer Edwards, **When Angels Cry**, (Yucca, 2014)

# About Lauren Kern

Lauren writes a large variety of stories, poems, and scripts as she balances athletics and schoolwork. She has been an avid writer since she was young, having been inspired by music, television, movies, and novels that provide the basis for her fiction and nonfiction works.

Scriptor has helped her develop her very first published work and transfer emotions from ink to paper while proudly creating and sharing her thoughts with the world in these unexpected times. These words give an insight into how Lauren perceives the way quarantine has shaped her life and others.

Currently, Lauren lives north of Chicago with her family and looks forward to further expanding her writing career.

# CHAPTER 8

# It Never Rains Forever

## by Brooke Holman

"How hard could it be?" they said.

"All you have to do is stay inside for a couple of weeks," they said.

What **they** didn't understand was how teens would react to this change.

Imagine sitting in your room thinking about seeing your friends at school the next day, or playing in your basketball game over the weekend, and then SNAP, it's all over. No more after-school trips to the sandwich shop with friends. No more volleyball practice with your favorite coach, and no more seeing the friends you love.

"Wow, that would suck," is what you're probably thinking.

Well, guess what? That is how me – along with millions of other teens all around the world – are feeling due to this fun little virus called COVID-19.

P.S. This virus is little.

But...

P.P.S. This virus is not fun... at all!

From my experience, I think teens are suffering from four main things during this quarantine: sadness, mental health issues, isolation, and unknowns.

## Sadness

This virus brought lots of sadness to teens. Many researchers agree that when a teen is going through puberty, their friends tend to be the most important to them. If that is true (and I think it is, because I'm going through it right now), being apart from our friends brings lots of unnecessary sadness and emotion into our already complicated lives. About 20% of teens suffer from depression, and I imagine that has spiked significantly during quarantine.

Then think about other factors impacting your life. For example, I have experienced some sad situations in my life recently, like my parents separating. This has led to a lot of stress and sadness in an already overwhelming quarantine.

## Mental Health

Common mental disorders like anxiety and depression have been much harder to deal with during quarantine. Social distancing means that all our normal support systems like friends, teachers, and counselors are unreachable. When my parents first separated, I was able to talk to my friends, teachers, and school counselors to get support. But now that there is a worldwide quarantine, that isn't possible. Due to this lack of touch and face-to-face interaction, millions of teens are suffering from depression and anxiety with no one to talk to.

"Well, what about parents?" some might ask.

That is where the term *they* comes in. *They* are the parents who tend to downplay the situation and say, "Just get over it. This will be over in a few months."

But a few months can seem like an eternity to a teen suffering from a mental health disorder. *They* are the politicians who say, "Look on the bright side," while enforcing unhelpful laws to separate people even more. *They* are the people who simply refuse to empathize with teens who are hurting.

## Isolation

How hard could it be? We just have to stay inside for a couple of weeks...or months...or years. Okay, I'm obviously getting a little ahead of myself. However, teens really are thinking like this right now. We are wondering when this is going to end! Many people think this is like a couple of months of vacation, but for teens, it's the opposite. We fuel ourselves by being outside, hanging out with friends, and doing new things. But none of these things can happen. Now our choices are limited to scrolling through TikTok, watching Netflix, and binge-eating. Fun, right? Nope. We have never been forced to stay inside with our family for this long, and it's really hard!

## Unknowns

What happens when you tell a kid, "I have a surprise for you."

The kid asks, "What is it?"

You respond, "I can't tell you until we get home."

The exasperated kid answers, "Are you kidding me? What is the point of telling me you have a surprise? First, it ruins the surprise, and second, it makes me anxious and curious."

That is the exact feeling teens have right now. We have no idea what is going to happen. Will the virus come to a random stop? Will we have a second strain that causes more destruction? Will unicorns fall from the sky, immediately curing the sick patients? We don't know! This creates a lot of anxiety in teens because we fear for the future.

## Solution

Now, the question you have all been wondering about: What can you do about all of this?

Although offering a quick fix like getting counseling or weekly check-ins may help, I think there is something more beneficial – adjusting your mindset. It is valuable to know things will always get better, and here are some analogies and sayings to help.

First, remember that life is 10% what happens to you and 90% how you handle it. Work on your own behavior and actions. You can't control the pandemic, but you can control the way you respond to it.

Second, imagine a pen with two ends representing good and bad things that happen to us. We need both ends of the pen in the same way that we need to embrace the good and bad times in life. When we focus on the positive end, we get more positives. When we focus on the negative end, we get more negative. The key is to keep a healthy balance to your emotions.

Third, be strong, because things will get better. It may be stormy now, but it never rains forever.

And last but not least, find ways to appreciate what you do have. It doesn't matter if the glass is half full or half empty – just be grateful that there's water in the cup. Drink it and stop complaining.

# About Brooke Holman

Brooke Holman is an outgoing young girl from Aspen, Colorado. She has wanted to learn more about emotions and mental health from a young age. Brooke's extreme feeling of empathy makes it seem as though you have known her for many years when you really just met.

Brooke's ability to turn difficult situations into positive experiences is amazing. She has plans to start a mental health club for teens at her school, publish a book of poetry, and to someday become a psychologist and businesswoman. Brooke's dreams are big, and her spirit is even bigger.

# CHAPTER 9

# It's All How You Look at It

**by Helen Treacy**

"**M**om, look! I finally found one," I shouted, my heart racing with excitement. I looked from the large patch of bright green heart-shaped clovers to the four-leaf clover in my palm. How was *I* able to find the lucky clover in a patch so crowded that my eyes could barely detect anything greater than a bright green blob? As I retraced my steps, I discovered a second four-leaf clover, and I grinned with joy.

On my first walk with my mom this quarantine, we stumbled across a thick patch of bright green clovers, some petite, some thumb-sized, and others crooked. My mom and I bent down, scrutinizing the patch for four-leaf clovers. A little luck would not hurt during this time of helplessness and uncertainty. My mom quickly found two four-leaf clovers – I felt like the bad luck charm.

"It is all about how you look," Mom suggested.

I shrugged off this advice because it didn't make much sense to me at the time. But my mom continued to find clovers and I still fell short, so I decided I might as well take her advice and began peering at these giant patches differently. I can't even describe my new mom-guided strategy, but my eyes led the way, and all of a sudden, I found my first four-leaf clover! A few seconds later, I found another! It felt great, like solving a complex riddle, finally finding the missing puzzle piece, or discovering a $20 bill in the pocket of an old jacket. It felt like luck. In a time when luck seemed elusive, I vowed to look for four-leaf clovers every chance I had. My point of view on luck shifted: "It's all about how you look at it."

When the stay-at-home order was announced, I felt an overwhelming surge of uncertainty and grief. I was not in control. Junior prom, spring lacrosse, and the excitement at the end of the school year were all canceled. I began to struggle at home. Shifting from a non-stop busy schedule to unclaimed time shocked me. The days merged together, and time ticked slowly away.

I missed school. I cherished the privilege of my education and missed "my second home." I suddenly longed to stay up late cramming for a test, and I missed the energy and buzz of my school hallways. That was when I decided to walk the dogs with my mom. I didn't even want to go at first, but Mom, watching me slowly become a couch potato, convinced me that a walk might not be such a painful prospect. I geared up and got ready. Our dog, Guinness, nipped at my feet, telling me to hurry up. I faced three-and-a-half miles of hilly terrain with trepidation, my mindset clouded with negativity not only about the walk I was about to endure but about everything I'd lost due to COVID-19.

As we started walking, the weather worsened my dejection. Clouds nestled themselves into our favorite walking place, the Presbyterian Home, which was once an orphanage and is now a stately home to cross country races and practices in the fall. On its grounds, many types of terrain encouraged all sorts of walks. But on this day, everything felt moody and abandoned. In the Pine Forest, needles crunched beneath my sneakers, reminding me of a crisp fall day when all was normal and calm. My breathing steadied. My daydream screeched to a sudden halt when my dog, Rosie, plopped herself into her favorite mud puddle. I couldn't help but laugh. My mom and I looked at our now-brown dog, mud smeared on her face. She seemed to laugh along with us, reminding me of the little things that busy life obscures. I took such joy in watching my dog make a great fool of herself and found comfort in having a great laugh with my mom. I felt a newfound pep in my step as I continued our walk with a giant smile across my face.

Mom and I continued on our normal loop, squeezing our way through a small entrance between two trees, past the green fishing pond to a hilly, maze-like field. We came upon another field with beautiful red barns and a horse show ring in the center. By now, the sun peeked out from behind the clouds, creating a kaleidoscope of welcoming shadows on the grass. Closer to the red barns, we noticed a large patch of green clovers. My mom, the "master" of finding four-leaf clovers, bent down and scanned the patch.

"Haha, I found one!" my mom bragged.

I gazed at her, unsure and overwhelmed. Hungry for a little extra luck, I studied the large patch.

"Found another!" Mom said, rubbing her luck into my face.

Sensing a little friendly competition, I couldn't let her win this hunt. Feeling silly as I crouched over, I doubted my own ability. "Mom, how do you even find these? I must be a bad luck charm because I don't see any," I complained.

"It's all about how you look," my mom whispered.

Her words mystified me. My mom maintained her luck, and I still was unable to find my own. "It's all about how you look" kept replaying in my head like a broken record. Suddenly, my eyes shifted and I began looking at these clovers a little differently. Shapes that once merged together began to separate, and my eyes were drawn to my first four-leaf clover. My heart bubbled with excitement.

I counted the leaves before rejoicing. "Mom, look! I finally found one," I exclaimed, handing her my clover so she could see for herself. She was proud of me and gently pressed my clovers against hers to help keep the leaves separated. I kept looking, and much to my surprise, my luck persisted. Soon I found a second four-leaf clover! For the first time in three weeks, I felt lucky. For the rest of the walk, I was on top of the world.

Mom and I continued walking daily, and I felt relieved that my mom never had an interest in discussing the pandemic. My mood was light-spirited, which allowed me to enjoy every moment of our walks. Even if the terrain was cloudy, the Presbyterian Home maintained an uplifting and welcoming mood.

On these walks, I realized all of the simple things I had been missing. The Pine Forest is beautiful and shields the animals that inhabit it from the sun. The large green pond houses various fish, turtles, and plants. And my personal favorite, the red barns, are home to the four-leaf clovers that changed my perspective of luck. Our walks allowed me to search a little deeper into nature and guided me to look at quarantine and life through a different lens. I realized that in the chaotic buzz of my everyday life before quarantine, I had been blinded from the simple moments that I should have treasured. "It's all about how you look at it" engraved itself into my mind and has continued to walk with me.

Everything we've taken for granted in life suddenly makes me ask, "What did I miss out on before?" The daily walks with my mom and creating memories with my family made me feel so lucky during quarantine. It has opened my eyes and helped me realize that materialistic things aren't what matter. Building deeper relationships with those closest to your heart does. Those relationships built and experiences created are the four-leaf clovers in life. Losing certain experiences due to COVID-19 was undeniably hard to manage, but it's all about *how you look at it*.

I think that's true about everything in life. Whenever you encounter something challenging, you have a choice to look at it differently. If you do, it might change everything. Be careful, you're going to miss them if you aren't looking. The four-leaf clovers are out there – you just need to look for them.

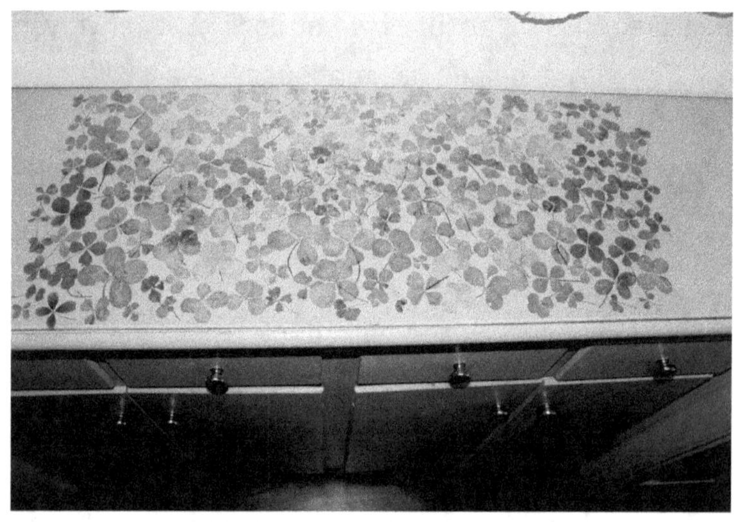

These are all the four-leaf clovers my mom and
I found during quarantine. We will keep looking.

# About Helen Treacy

Helen is an active high school student who (outside quarantine) stays busy with academics, athletics, leadership roles, and spending quality time with family and friends. She has always had a passion for expressing herself through writing. She has a mature outlook on the world around her and is perceptive of her environment and human nature, which comes through in her writing.

Helen has thoroughly enjoyed her experience with the teen writing project and hopes to pursue creative writing in the future.

Helen lives in Central Virginia with her family, two dogs, and a cat.

# Proceeds from this book
# will be donated to:

# The Center for Disease Philanthropy
# (CDP) COVID-19 Response Fund

(https://disasterphilanthropy.org/cdp-fund/cdp-covid-19-response-fund/)

AND

# Doctors Without Borders

(www.doctorswithoutborders.org)

# WANT TO BE
# A PUBLISHED AUTHOR?

Scriptor Publishing Group offers services including writing, publishing, marketing and consulting to take your book...

## *From Dream to Published!*

Email us at
info@scriptorpublishinggroup.com
to get started!